Alfred's Easy ukulele songs
ROCK and POP

50 HITS FROM ACROSS THE DECADES

Alfred

Produced by
Alfred Music
P.O. Box 10003
Van Nuys, CA 91410-0003
alfred.com

Printed in USA.

No part of this book shall be reproduced, arranged, adapted, recorded, publicly performed, stored in a retrieval system,
or transmitted by any means without written permission from the publisher. In order to comply with copyright laws, please apply for
such written permission and/or license by contacting the publisher at alfred.com/permissions.

ISBN-10: 1-4706-2603-9
ISBN-13: 978-1-4706-2603-7

Cover Photo
Maestro Mango Tenor ukulele courtesy of Your Perfect Guitar, yourperfectguitar.com. Photographed by Arun Palaniappa

 Alfred Cares. Contents printed on environmentally responsible paper.

artist index

contents

TITLE	ARTIST	

STRUM PATTERNS

Below are a number of suggested patterns that may be used while strumming the chords for the songs in this book. Think of these as starting points from which you may embellish, mix up, or create your own patterns.

Note the markings above the staff that indicate the direction of the strums.

☐ = indicates a downstroke

V = indicates an upstroke

6

AIN'T MISBEHAVIN'

Words by
ANDY RAZAF

Music by
THOMAS "FATS" WALLER
and HARRY BROOKS

Use Suggested Strum Pattern #14

Slow swing

© 1929 (Renewed) EMI MILLS MUSIC INC., CHAPPELL & CO., INC. and RAZAF MUSIC CO.
All Rights Reserved

BAD TO THE BONE

Suggested Strum Pattern: See bars 1 and 2

Words and Music by
GEORGE THOROGHGOOD

1. On the day I was born, nurs-es all gath-ered 'round,
2.3. *See additional lyrics*

and they gazed in wide won-der at the joy they had found.

The head nurse spoke up, said, "Leave this one a-lone."

She could tell right a-way I was bad to the bone.

Bad to the bone. Bad to the bone.

Bad to the Bone - 2 - 1

© 1981, 1982 DEL SOUND MUSIC
All Rights Reserved

B - b - b - b - b - bad.___   B - b - b - b - b - bad.___

1.2.

B - b - b - b - b - bad,___   bad___ to the bone.

3.

bad___ to the bone.

N.C.

Verse 2:
I broke a thousand hearts
Before I met you.
I'll break a thousand more, baby,
Before I am through.
I wanna be yours, pretty baby,
Yours and yours alone.
I'm here to tell ya, honey,
That I'm bad to the bone,
Bad to the bone.
B-b-b-b-b-b-b bad,
B-b-b-b-b-b-b bad.
B-b-b-b-b-b-b bad,
Bad to the bone.
(To Guitar Solo:)

Verse 3:
Now, when I walk the streets,
Kings and Queens step aside.
Every woman I meet, heh, heh,
They all stay satisfied.
I wanna tell you, pretty baby,
What I see I make my own.
And I'm here to tell ya, honey,
That I'm bad to the bone,
Bad to the bone.
B-b-b-b-b-b-b bad,
B-b-b-b-b-b-b bad.
B-b-b-b-b-b-b bad,
Whoo, bad to the bone.

BIG YELLOW TAXI

Use Suggested Strum Pattern #2

Words and Music by
JONI MITCHELL

1. They paved par - a - dise,___ put up a park - ing lot.___
2.3.4. *See additional lyrics*

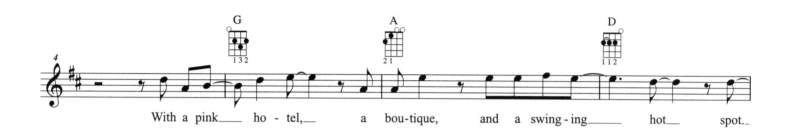

With a pink___ ho - tel,___ a bou - tique, and a swing - ing___ hot___ spot.___

Chorus:

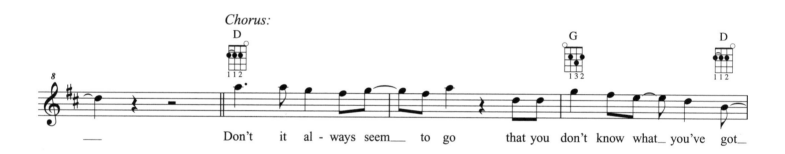

___ Don't it al - ways seem___ to go that you don't know what___ you've got___

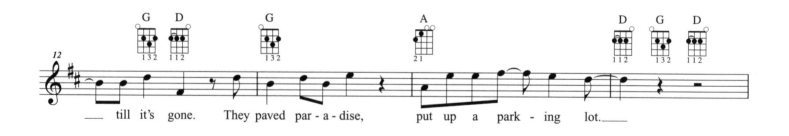

___ till it's gone. They paved par - a - dise, put up a park - ing lot.___

1.2.3. **4.**

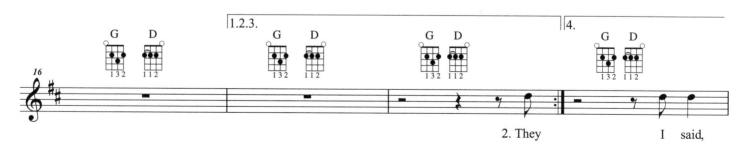

2. They I said,

Big Yellow Taxi - 2 - 1

© 1970 (Renewed) CRAZY CROW MUSIC.
All Rights Administered by SONY/ATV MUSIC PUBLISHING, 8 Music Square West, Nashville, TN 37203
All Rights Reserved

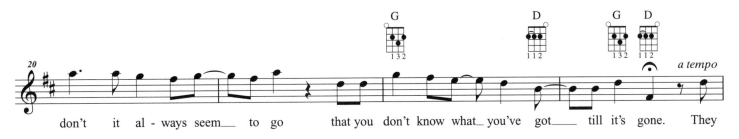

don't it al - ways seem— to go that you don't know what— you've got—— till it's gone. They

paved par - a - dise, put up a park - ing lot.—— They

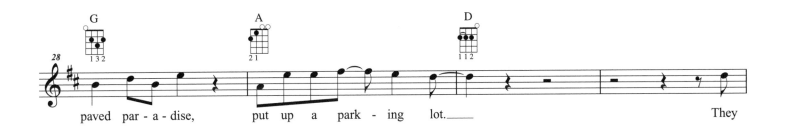

paved par - a - dise, put up a park - ing lot.—— They

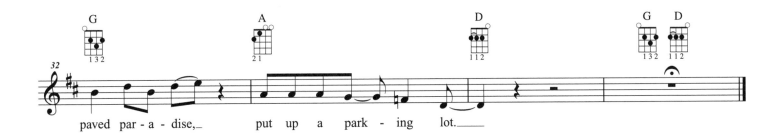

paved par - a - dise,— put up a park - ing lot.——

Verse 2:
They took all the trees
Put 'em in a tree museum
And they charged the people
A dollar and a half just to see 'em
(To Chorus:)

Verse 3:
Hey, farmer, farmer
Put away that D.D.T. now
Give me spots on my apples
But leave me the birds and the bees. Please
(To Chorus:)

Verse 4:
Late last night
I heard the screen door slam
And a big yellow taxi
Took away my old man
(To Chorus:)

BLUE MOON

Use Suggested Strum Pattern #3

Moderately

Music by RICHARD RODGERS
Lyrics by LORENZ HART

Blue Moon - 3 - 1

© 1934 (Renewed) METRO-GOLDWYN-MAYER INC.
All Rights Controlled and Administered by EMI ROBBINS CATALOG INC. (Publishing) and ALFRED MUSIC (Print)
All Rights Reserved

14

BOTH SIDES NOW

Use Suggested Strum Pattern #3

Moderately

Words and Music by
JONI MITCHELL

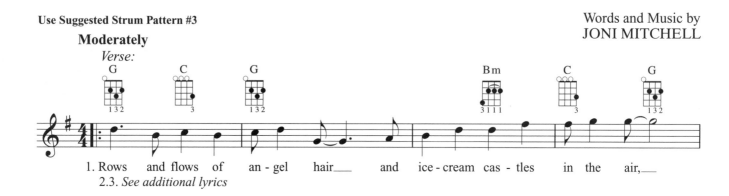

1. Rows and flows of an-gel hair___ and ice-cream cas-tles in the air,___
2.3. *See additional lyrics*

and feath-er can - yons ev - 'ry-where. I've looked at clouds that way. But

now they on - ly block the sun,___ they rain and snow on ev - 'ry - one.___

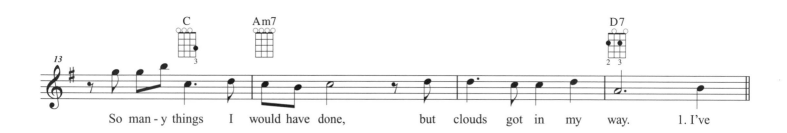

So man - y things I would have done, but clouds got in my way. 1. I've

Chorus:

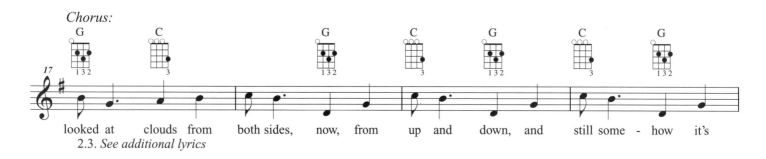

looked at clouds from both sides, now, from up and down, and still some - how it's
2.3. *See additional lyrics*

Both Sides Now - 2 - 1

© 1967 (Renewed) CRAZY CROW MUSIC
All Rights Excluding Print Administered by SONY/ATV MUSIC PUBLISHING, 8 Music Square West, Nashville, TN 37203
Exclusive Print Rights Administered by ALFRED MUSIC
All Rights Reserved

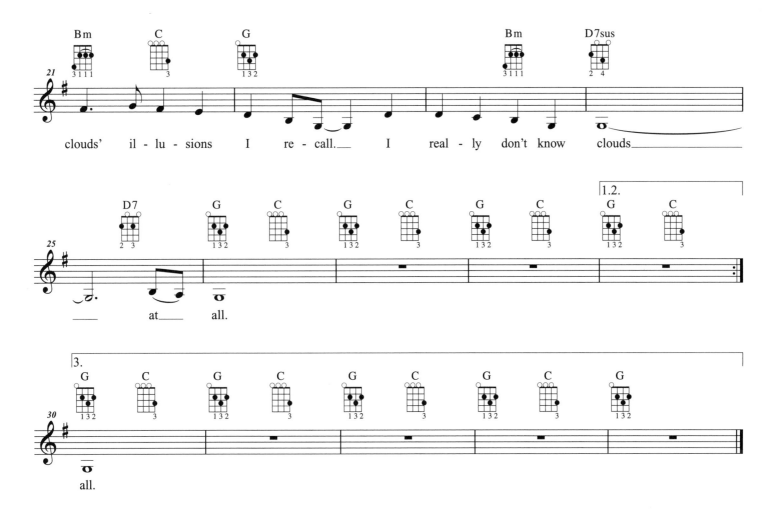

clouds' il - lu - sions I re - call.___ I real - ly don't know clouds___

at___ all.

all.

Verse 2:
Moons and Junes and Ferris wheels
The dizzy dancing way you feel
When every fairy tale comes real
I've looked at love that way
But now it's just another show
You leave 'em laughing when you go
And if you care, don't let them know
Don't give yourself away

Chorus 2:
I've looked at love from both sides, now
From win and lose, and still somehow
It's love's illusions I recall
I really don't know love at all

Verse 3:
Tears and fears and feeling proud
To say "I love you" right out loud
Dreams and schemes and circus crowds
I've looked at life that way
But now old friends are acting strange
They shake their heads, they say I've changed
Well, something's lost but something's gained
In living every day

Chorus 3:
I've looked at life from both sides, now
From win and lose, and still somehow
It's life's illusions I recall
I really don't know life at all

BROWN SUGAR

Words and Music by
MICK JAGGER and KEITH RICHARDS

Use Suggested Strum Pattern #2

Moderately

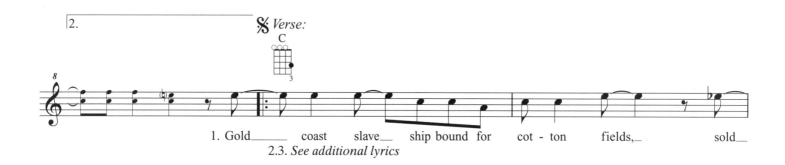

1. Gold____ coast slave__ ship bound for cot - ton fields,__ sold__
2.3. *See additional lyrics*

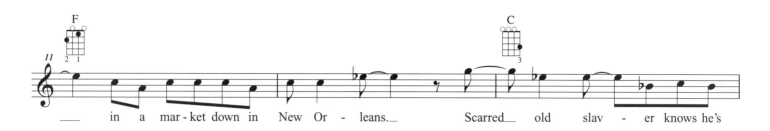

____ in a mar - ket down in New Or - leans.__ Scarred__ old slav - er knows he's

do'n' - al - right,__ hear____ him whip the wom - en just____ a - round mid - night.

Brown Sugar - 3 - 1

© 1971 (Renewed) ABKCO MUSIC, INC., 85 Fifth Avenue, New York, NY 10003
All Rights Reserved

Verse 2:
Drums beating, cold English blood runs hot,
Lady of the house wondrin' where it's gonna stop.
House boy knows that he's doin' alright,
You should a heard him just around midnight.
(To Chorus:)

Verse 3:
I bet your mama was a tent show queen,
And all her boyfriends were sweet sixteen.
I'm no schoolboy but I know what I like,
You should have heard me just around midnight.
(To Chorus:)

BYE BYE BLACKBIRD

Words by
MORT DIXON **Use Suggested Strum Pattern #14**

Music by
RAY HENDERSON

© 1926 (Renewed) RAY HENDERSON MUSIC COMPANY and OLDE CLOVER LEAF MUSIC
All Rights Reserved

CHAIN GANG

Words and Music by
SAM COOKE

© 1960 (Renewed) ABKCO MUSIC, INC., 85 Fifth Avenue, New York, NY 10003
All Rights Reserved

23

Chain Gang - 3 - 2

CHANGES IN LATITUDES, CHANGES IN ATTITUDES

**Use Suggested
Strum Pattern #6
Moderately**

Words and Music by
JIMMY BUFFETT

© 1977 CORAL REEFER MUSIC and OUTER BANKS MUSIC
All Rights Administered by CORAL REEFER MUSIC
All Rights Reserved

Verse 2:
Reading departure signs in some big airport
Reminds me of the places I've been.
Visions of good times that brought so much pleasure
Makes me want to go back again.
If it suddenly ended tomorrow,
I could somehow adjust to the fall.
Good times and riches and son of a bitches,
I've seen more than I can recall.

Chorus 2:
These changes in latitudes,
Changes in attitudes;
Nothing remains quite the same.
Through all of the islands and all of the highlands,
If we couldn't laugh we would all go insane.

Verse 3:
I think about Paris when I'm high on red wine;
I wish I could jump on a plane.
And so many nights I just dream of the ocean.
God, I wish I was sailin' again.
Oh, yesterdays are over my shoulder,
So I can't look back for too long.
There's just too much to see waiting in front of me,
And I know that I just can't go wrong.

Chorus 3:
With these changes in latitudes,
Changes in attitudes;
Nothing remains quite the same.
With all of my running and all of my cunning,
If I couldn't laugh I would all go insane.
(To Coda)

Changes in Latitudes, Changes in Attitudes - 2 - 2

COLOUR MY WORLD

Words and Music by
JAMES PANKOW

As time goes on_____ I re-al-ize just what you

mean_____ to_____ me. And now,_____ now that you're

near prom-ise your love that I've wait-ed to share._____ And

dreams of our mo-ments to-geth - er_____ col-our my world_____ with

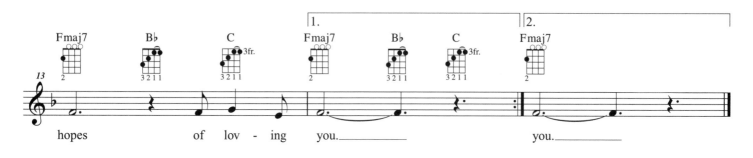

hopes of lov-ing you._____ 1. 2. you._____

© 1970 (Renewed) SPIRIT CATALOG HOLDINGS, S.à.r.l. and LAMMINATIONS MUSIC
US, UK and Canadian Rights for SPIRIT CATALOGUE HOLDINGS, S.à.r.l. Controlled and Administered by SPIRIT TWO MUSIC, INC.
Rights for the Rest of World are Controlled and Administered by SPIRIT SERVICES HOLDINGS, S.à.r.l. on behalf of SPIRIT CATALOGUE HOLDINGS, S.à.r.l.
All Rights Reserved

COOL KIDS

Words and Music by
GRAHAM SIEROTA, JAMIE SIEROTA,
NOAH SIEROTA, SYDNEY SIEROTA,
JEFFERY DAVID SIEROTA and
JESIAH DZWONEK

Use Suggested Strum Pattern #1 (all downstrokes)

Moderately

Cool Kids - 3 - 1

© 2013 WB MUSIC CORP., ECHOSMITH SONGS, REACH GLOBAL (UK) LTD., JEFFERY DAVID SONGS and CRANBERRY ROAD PUBLISHING
All Rights on behalf of Itself and ECHOSMITH SONGS Administered by WB MUSIC CORP.
All Rights Reserved

30

they seem to fit in. I wish that I could be like the cool kids, like the cool kids."

1.

D Em Cmaj7 G D

Em Cmaj7 G D D 2.

2. He sees them ___

Chorus:

Em Cmaj7 G D

"I wish that I could be like the cool kids, 'cause all the cool kids, they seem to fit in.

Em Cmaj7 G D

I wish that I could be like the cool kids, like the cool kids."___

Interlude:

Em Cmaj7 G D

Em Cmaj7 G D

And they said,

DANCING QUEEN

Words and Music by
BENNY ANDERSSON, STIG ANDERSON
and BJORN ULVAEUS

Use Suggested Strum Pattern #6

Dancing Queen - 2 - 1

© 1976 (Renewed) POLAR MUSIC AB (Sweden)
All Rights in the U.S. and Canada Administered by EMI GROVE PARK MUSIC, INC. and UNIVERSAL-SONGS OF POLYGRAM INTERNATIONAL, INC.
Exclusive Print Rights for EMI GROVE PARK MUSIC INC. Administered by ALFRED MUSIC
All Rights for UK/Eire Administered by BOCU MUSIC LTD.
All Rights Reserved

DO YOU WANT TO KNOW A SECRET

Use Suggested Strum Pattern #4
Slowly

Words and Music by
JOHN LENNON and
PAUL McCARTNEY

© 1963 (Renewed) NORTHERN SONGS LTD. (UK)
All Rights in the U.S. and Canada Controlled by EMI UNART CATALOG INC. (Publishing) and ALFRED MUSIC (Print)
All Rights Reserved

DON'T STOP BELIEVIN'

Use Suggested Strum Pattern #2

Moderately

Intro:

Words and Music by
JONATHAN CAIN, NEAL SCHON
and STEVE PERRY

Verse 1:

Just a small town girl,___ liv-in' in a lone-ly world.___

She took the mid-night train___ go-in' an-y - where.___

Just a cit-y boy,___ born and raised in South De-troit.___

He took the mid-night train___ go-in' an-y - where.___

Don't Stop Believin' - 3 - 1

© 1981 WEEDHIGH-NIGHTMARE MUSIC and LACEY BOULEVARD MUSIC
All Rights for WEEDHIGH-NIGHTMARE MUSIC Administered by WIXEN MUSIC PUBLISHING INC.
All Rights Reserved

Verse 2:

A sin-ger in a smok-y room,_ a smell of wine_ and cheap per-fume.__

For a smile_ they can share the night;_ it__ goes on and on__ and on__ and on.__

Bridge:

Strang - ers__ wait - ing__ up and down the boul - e - vard._ Their

To Coda

shad - ows__ search - ing__ in the night._____

Street - lights,_ peo - ple,__ liv - ing just to find e - mo - tion.

Hid - ing__ some - where_ in the night._____

EASY TO BE HARD

Use Suggested Strum Pattern #6

Moderately slow

Music by GALT MacDERMOT
Words by JAMES RADO and GEROME RAGNI

Easy to Be Hard - 2 - 1

© 1966, 1967, 1968 1970 (Copyrights Renewed) JAMES RADO, GEROME RAGNI, GALT MacDERMOT, NAT SHAPIRO and EMI U CATALOG, INC.
All Rights Controlled and Administered by EMI U CATALOG INC. (Publishing) and ALFRED MUSIC (Print)
All Rights Reserved

EVERYTHING IS AWESOME
(Awesome Remixxx!!!)
(from *The Lego Movie*)

Lyrics by
SHAWN PATTERSON, ANDY SAMBERG,
AKIVA SCHAFFER, JORMA TACCONE,
JOSHUA BARTHOLOMEW and LISA HARRITON

Music by
SHAWN PATTERSON

Use Suggested Strum Pattern #1
Moderately fast

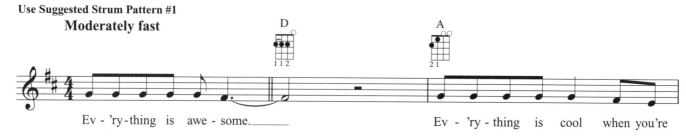

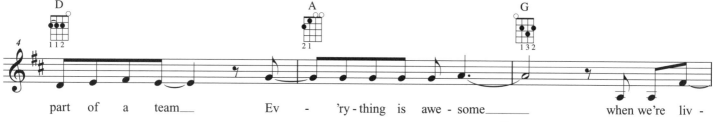

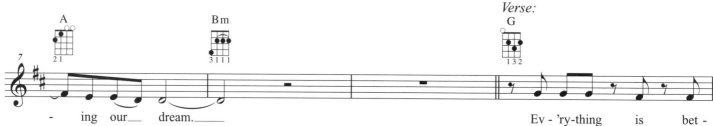

Everything Is Awesome (Awesome Remixxx!!!) - 3 - 1

© 2014 WARNER-OLIVE MUSIC LLC, DROHNEND PUBLISHING, SHEBAR MUSIC, BONER TEK and SNUGLAR ENTERTAINMENT
Exclusive Worldwide Print Rights for WARNER-OLIVE MUSIC LLC Administered by ALFRED MUSIC
All Rights Reserved

42

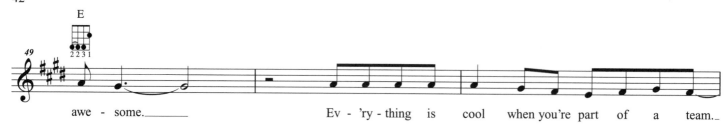

awe - some._____   Ev - 'ry-thing is cool when you're part of a team.__

___ Ev - 'ry-thing is awe - some_____ when we're liv - ing our__ dream.

Rap Section 2:   *Play 4 times*

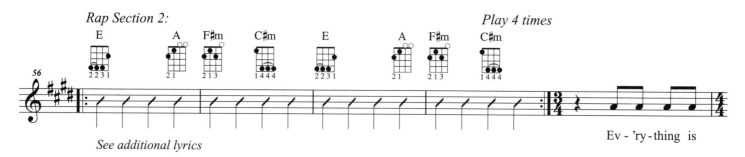

See additional lyrics

Ev - 'ry-thing is

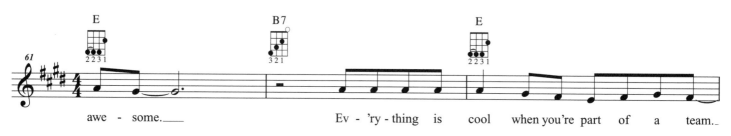

awe - some.___   Ev - 'ry-thing is cool when you're part of a team._

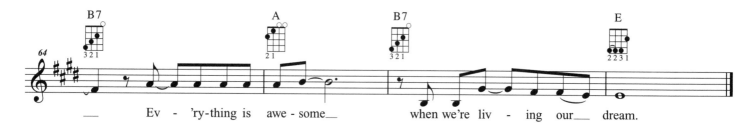

___ Ev - 'ry-thing is awe - some_____ when we're liv - ing our__ dream.

Rap section 1:
Have you heard the news, everyone's talking
Life is good 'cause everything's awesome
Lost my job, it's a new opportunity
More free time for my awesome community.

I feel more awesome than an awesome possum
Dip my body in chocolate frostin'
Three years later, wash off the frostin'
Smellin' like a blossom, everything is awesome
Stepped in mud, got new brown shoes
It's awesome to win, and it's awesome to lose (it's awesome to lose).

Rap section 2:
Blue skies, bouncy springs
We just named two awesome things
A Nobel prize, a piece of string
You know what's awesome? EVERYTHING!

Dogs with fleas, allergies,
A book of Greek antiquities
Brand new pants, a very old vest
Awesome items are the best.

Trees, frogs, clogs
They're awesome
Rocks, clocks, and socks
They're awesome
Figs, and jigs, and twigs
That's awesome
Everything you see, or think, or say
Is awesome.

FALLING SLOWLY

(from *Once*)

Use Suggested Strum Pattern #1

Words and Music by
GLEN HANSARD and
MARKETA IRGLOVA

Slowly

Verse:

1. I don't know you, but I want you all the more for that.
2. Fall - ing slow - ly, eyes that know me all and I can't go back.

Words fall through me and al - ways fool me
Words that take me____ and e - rase me

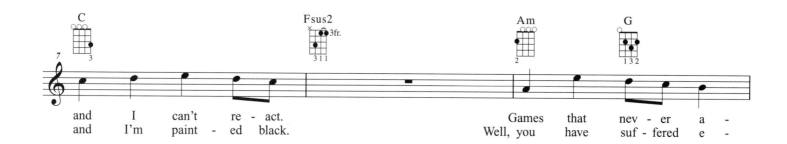

and I can't re - act. Games that nev - er a -
and I'm paint - ed black. Well, you have suf - fered e -

mount to more than they're meant will play them-selves out.___ }
nough and warred with your - self. It's time that you won.___ }

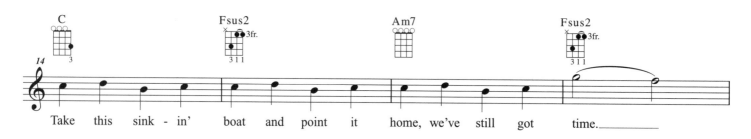

Take this sink - in' boat and point it home, we've still got time._____

Falling Slowly - 2 - 1

© 2006 THE SWELL SEASON PUBLISHING (ASCAP)
All Rights Administered by WB MUSIC CORP. (ASCAP)
Exclusive Worldwide Print Rights Administered by ALFRED MUSIC
All Rights Reserved

FERNANDO

Words and Music by
BENNY ANDERSSON, STIG ANDERSON
and BJORN ULVAEUS

Use Suggested Strum Pattern #3

Moderately

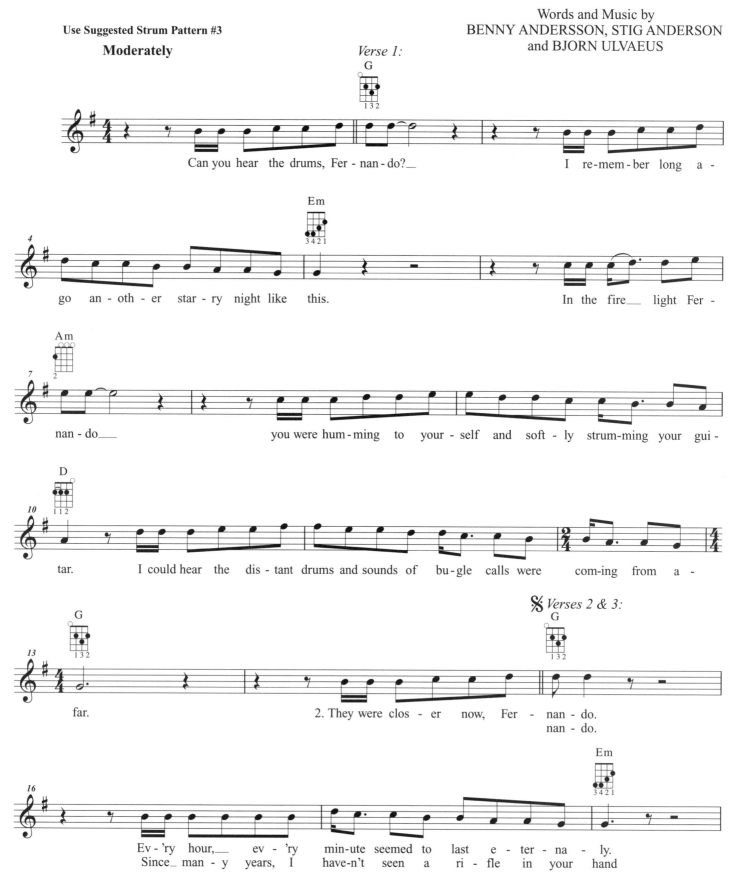

Fernando - 3 - 1

© 1976 (Renewed) UNION SONGS AB (Sweden)
All Rights in the U.S. and Canada Administered by EMI GROVE PARK MUSIC INC. and UNIVERSAL-SONGS OF POLYGRAM INTERNATIONAL, INC.
Exclusive Print Rights for EMI GROVE PARK MUSIC, INC. Administered by ALFRED MUSIC
All Rights for UK/Eire Administered by BOCU MUSIC LTD.
All Rights Reserved

my friend, Fer - nan - do.   If I had to do the same a - gain, I would,_

my friend, Fer - nan - do.   3. Now we're old and gray, Fer -

There was some-thing in the air that night._ The stars_ were bright,_ Fer - nan-

- do.   They were shin - ing there for you and me,_ for lib - er - ty_ Fer - nan-

- do.   Though we nev - er thought that we could lose,_ there's no re - gret._

If I had to do the same a - gain,_ I would,_ my friend,_ Fer - nan - do.

If I had to do the same a - gain,_ I would,_ my friend,_ Fer - nan - do.

FORGET YOU

Words and Music by
CHRISTOPHER BROWN, PHILIP LAWRENCE, ARI LEVINE,
BRUNO MARS and THOMAS CALLAWAY

Use Suggested Strum Pattern #6

Moderately bright

Forget You - 3 - 1

© 2010 NORTHSIDE INDEPENDENT MUSIC PUBLISHING LLC, THOU ART THE HUNGER,
WESTSIDE INDEPENDENT MUSIC PUBLISHING LLC, LATE 80'S MUSIC, WB MUSIC CORP., ROC NATION MUSIC,
MUSIC FAMAMANEM, ROUND HILL SONGS, BUGHOUSE, MARS FORCE MUSIC, and CHRYSALIS MUSIC LTD.
All Rights on behalf of itself and THOU ART THE HUNGER Administered by NORTHSIDE INDEPENDENT MUSIC PUBLISHING LLC
All Rights on behalf of itself and LATE 80'S MUSIC Administered by WESTSIDE INDEPENDENT MUSIC PUBLISHING LLC
All Rights for BUGHOUSE and MARS FORCE MUSIC Administered by BUG MUSIC/BMG RIGHTS MANAGEMENT (US) LLC
All Rights on behalf of itself and ROC NATION MUSIC and MUSIC FAMAMANEM Administered by WB MUSIC CORP.
All Rights Reserved

GHOSTBUSTERS

Words and Music by
RAY PARKER, JR.

Use Suggested Strum Pattern #4

Moderately

Intro:

Play 3 times

Ghost - bust - ers!   1. If there's

Verses 1 & 2:

some - thing strange   in your neigh - bor - hood.
see - ing things   run - ning through your head.

(1.) Who you gon - na call?   Ghost - bust - ers!   { If there's
(2.) Who can you call? }   { An in -
3. *See additional lyrics*

some - thing weird,   and it don't look good. }
vis - i - ble man   sleep - ing in your bed. }

Who you gon - na call?   Ghost - bust - ers!

© 1984 EMI GOLDEN TORCH MUSIC CORP. and RAYDIOLA MUSIC
Exclusive Print Rights for EMI GOLDEN TORCH MUSIC CORP. Administered by ALFRED MUSIC
All Rights Reserved

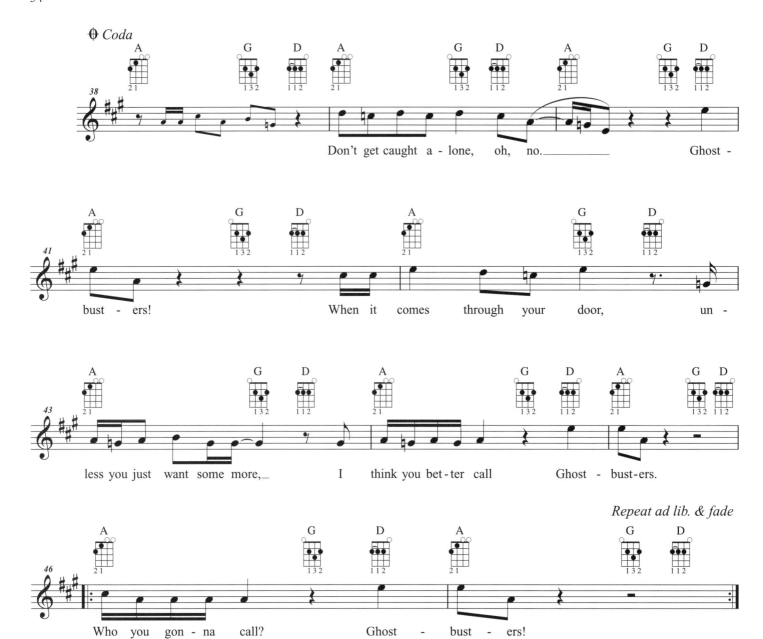

Verse 3:
Who you gonna call?
Ghostbusters!
If you've had a dose of a freaky ghost,
Baby, you'd better call...
Ghostbusters!
Let me tell you something,
Bustin' makes me feel good.
I ain't afraid of no ghost.
I ain't afraid of no ghost.
(To Coda)

GREATEST LOVE OF ALL

Words by
LINDA CREED

Music by
MICHAEL MASSER

Use Suggested Strum Pattern #4

Moderately, with a half-time feel

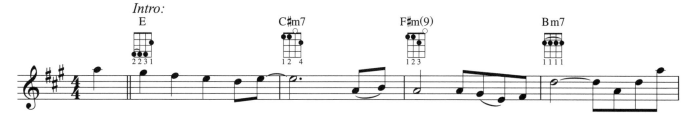

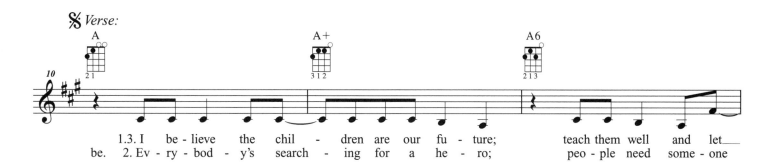

1.3. I be-lieve the chil-dren are our fu-ture; teach them well and let___
be. 2. Ev-ry-bod-y's search-ing for a he-ro; peo-ple need some-one

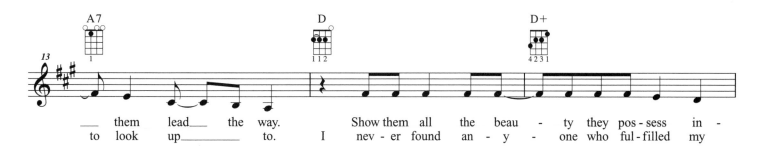

___ them lead___ the way. Show them all the beau-ty they pos-sess into look up_____ to. I nev-er found an-y-one who ful-filled my

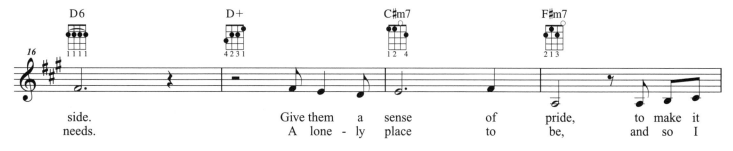

side. Give them a sense of pride, to make it
needs. A lone-ly place to be, and so I

Greatest Love of All - 3 - 1

© 1977 (Renewed) EMI GOLD HORIZON MUSIC CORP. and EMI GOLDEN TORCH MUSIC CORP.
Exclusive Print Rights Administered by ALFRED MUSIC
All Rights Reserved

GRENADE

Use Suggested Strum Pattern #6

Words and Music by
CLAUDE KELLY, BRODY BROWN, PHILIP LAWRENCE,
ARI LEVINE, ANDREW WYATT and BRUNO MARS

Moderately

Grenade - 3 - 1

© 2010 WB MUSIC CORP., WARNER-TAMERLANE PUBLISHING CORP., STUDIO BEAST MUSIC, NORTHSIDE INDEPENDENT MUSIC PUBLISHING LLC,
THOU ART THE HUNGER, WESTSIDE INDEPENDENT MUSIC PUBLISHING, LATE 80'S MUSIC, ROC NATION MUSIC, MUSIC FAMAMANEM,
ROUND HILL SONGS, DOWNTOWN COPYRIGHT MANAGEMENT LLC, BUGHOUSE and MARS FORCE MUSIC
All Rights on behalf of itself and STUDIO BEAST MUSIC Administered by WARNER-TAMERLANE PUBLISHING CORP.
All Rights on behalf of itself and THOU ART THE HUNGER Administered by NORTHSIDE INDEPENDENT MUSIC PUBLISHING LLC
All Rights on behalf of itself and LATE 80'S MUSIC Administered by WESTSIDE INDEPENDENT MUSIC PUBLISHING LLC
All Rights on behalf of itself, ROC NATION MUSIC and MUSIC FAMAMANEM Administered by WB MUSIC CORP.
All Rights for BUGHOUSE and MARS FORCE MUSIC Administered by BUG MUSIC/BMG RIGHTS MANAGEMENT (US) LLC
All Rights Reserved

Verse 2:
Black, black, black and blue, beat me 'til I'm numb.
Tell the devil I said, "Hey" when you get back to where you're from.
Mad woman, bad woman, that's just what you are.
Yeah, you'll smile in my face then rip the brakes out my car.
(To Chorus:)

I CAN SEE CLEARLY NOW

Use Suggested Strum Pattern #7

Moderate reggae

Words and Music by
JOHNNY NASH

1.3. I can see clear - ly now___ the rain___ is gone.___
2. Think I can make___ it now___ the pain___ is gone.___

I can see all_____ ob - sta - cles
All of the bad_____ feel - ings have

in my way.___ Gone are the dark
dis - ap - peared.___ Here is the rain -

___ clouds___ that had___ me blind.___ } It's gon-na be a
- bow I've___ been pray - ing for.___ }

To Coda ⊕

bright, (Bright,_) bright___ (bright) sun - shin - y day.

1.

It's gon-na be a bright, (Bright,_) bright___ (bright) sun - shin - y day.___

I Can See Clearly Now - 2 - 1

© 1972 (Renewed) NASHCO MUSIC
All Rights for the World Outside of North America Administered by WARNER/CHAPPELL MUSIC, INC.
All Rights Reserved

I SAW HER STANDING THERE

Use Suggested Strum Pattern #1

Moderately fast

Words and Music by
JOHN LENNON and PAUL McCARTNEY

1. Well, she was

Verses 1 & 2:

just sev-en-teen,___ you know what I mean.___ And the
she looked at me,___ and I, I could see___ that be-

way she looked_ was way be-yond com-pare.___ }
bore too long_ I'd fall in love with her.___ }

So

how could I_ dance with an-oth-er.___ Oh! When I

1.
2.

saw her stand-ing there. 2. Well, Well, my

% *Bridge:*

heart went boom___ when I crossed that room___ and I

I Saw Her Standing There - 2 - 1

© 1963 (Renewed) NORTHERN SONGS, LTD (PRS)
All Rights in the United States of America, its territories and possessions and Canada
Assigned to and Controlled by ROUND HILL WORKS (BMI) on behalf of GIL MUSIC CORP. (BMI)
All Rights Reserved

IF YOU LEAVE ME NOW

Use Suggested Strum Pattern #6

Moderately slow

Words and Music by
PETER CETERA

Intro:

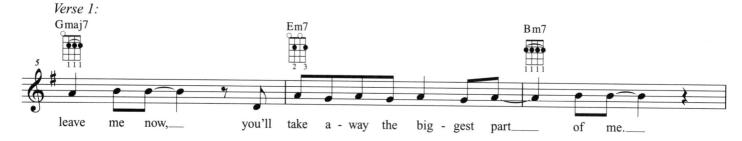

If you

Verse 1:

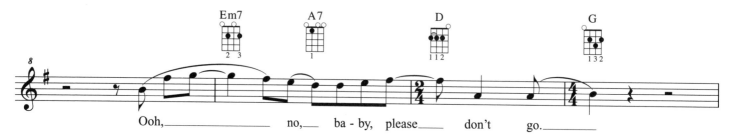

leave me now,___ you'll take a - way the big - gest part___ of me.___

Ooh,___ no,___ ba - by, please___ don't go.___

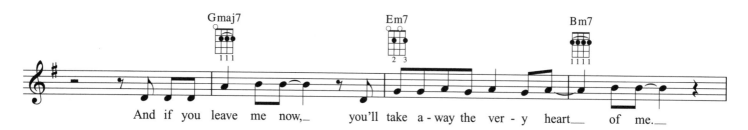

And if you leave me now,___ you'll take a - way the ver - y heart___ of me.___

Ooh,___ no,___ ba - by, please___ don't go.___ Ooh,___

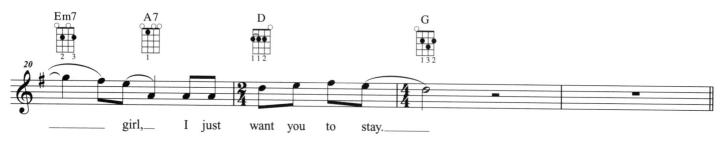

___ girl,___ I just want you to stay.___

If You Leave Me Now - 3 - 1

© 1976 (Renewed) SPIRIT CATALOG HOLDINGS, S.à.r.l. and UNIVERSAL MUSIC–MGB SONGS
U.S., UK and Canadian Rights for SPIRIT CATALOGUE HOLDINGS, S.à.r.l. Controlled and Administered by SPIRIT TWO MUSIC, INC. (ASCAP)
All Rights for the Rest of World are Controlled and Administered by SPIRIT SERVICES HOLDINGS, S.à.r.l.
on behalf of SPIRIT CATALOGUE HOLDINGS, S.à.r.l.
All Rights Reserved   Used by Permission

If You Leave Me Now - 3 - 2

68

If You Leave Me Now - 3 - 3

IT DON'T MEAN A THING
(If It Ain't Got That Swing)

Words by
IRVING MILLS

Music by
DUKE ELLINGTON

Fast swing A

Use Suggested
Strum Pattern #14

It don't mean a thing if it ain't got that swing,___ doo wah,___ doo wah, doo wah, doo wah, doo wah,___ doo wah, doo wah, doo wah. It don't mean a thing, all you got to do is sing, doo wah,___ doo wah, doo wah, doo wah, doo wah,___ doo wah, doo wah, doo wah. It makes no dif-'rence if___ it's sweet or hot;___ just give that rhy-thm ev-'ry thing you got. It don't mean a thing if it ain't got that swing,___ doo wah,___ doo wah, doo wah, doo wah, doo wah,___

1. ___ doo wah, doo wah, doo wah. It

2. ___ doo wah, doo wah, doo wah.

© 1932 (Renewed) EMI MILLS MUSIC, INC. and SONY/ATV MUSIC PUBLISHING LLC
Exclusive Print Rights for EMI MILLS MUSIC, INC. Administered by ALFRED MUSIC
All Rights Reserved

JUMPIN' JACK FLASH

Words and Music by
MICK JAGGER and KEITH RICHARDS

Use Suggested Strum Pattern #6

© 1968 (Renewed) ABKCO MUSIC, INC., 85 Fifth Avenue, New York, NY 10003
All Rights Reserved

now, in fact, it's a gas!___ But it's all_____ right, I'm

Jump-in' Jack Flash, it's a gas! Gas! Gas!_

Outro:

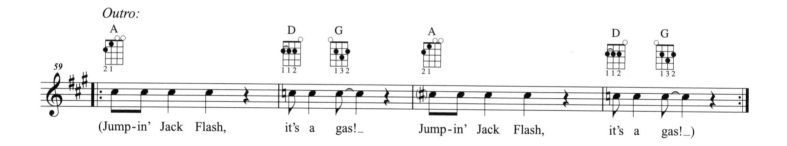

(Jump-in' Jack Flash, it's a gas!_ Jump-in' Jack Flash, it's a gas!_)

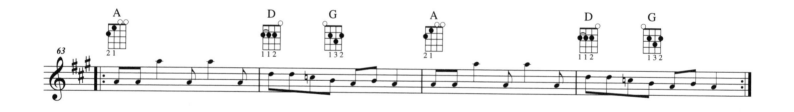

Verse 3:
I was drowned, I was washed up and left for dead.
I fell down to my feet and I saw they bled.
I frowned at the crumbs of a crust of bread.
I was crowned with a spike right thru my head.
(To Chorus:)

JUST THE WAY YOU ARE (AMAZING)

Use Suggested Strum Pattern #2

Moderately

Words and Music by
KHALIL WALTON, PETER HERNANDEZ,
PHILIP LAWRENCE, ARI LEVINE
and KHARI CAIN

Just the Way You Are (Amazing) - 3 - 1

© 2010 WB MUSIC CORP., UPPER DEC, ROC NATION MUSIC, MUSIC FAMAMANEM, NORTHSIDE INDEPENDENT MUSIC PUBLISHING LLC,
ROUND HILL SONGS, BUGHOUSE, MARS FORCE MUSIC, UNIVERSAL MUSIC CORP. and DRY RAIN ENTERTAINMENT
All Rights on behalf of itself, UPPER DEC, ROC NATION MUSIC and MUSIC FAMAMANEM Administered by WB MUSIC CORP.
All Rights for BUGHOUSE and MARS FORCE MUSIC Administered by BUG MUSIC/BMG RIGHTS MANAGEMENT (US) LLC
All Rights on behalf of itself and DRY RAIN ENTERTAINMENT Controlled and Administered by UNIVERSAL MUSIC CORP.
All Rights Reserved

LEAVING ON A JET PLANE

Words and Music by
JOHN DENVER

Use Suggested Strum Pattern #2

Moderately   *Verse:*

1. All my bags are packed,__ I'm read-y to go, I'm stand-ing here__ out-
man-y times__ I've let__ you down, so man-y times__ I've
3. Now the time__ has come to leave you; one more time__ let

side your door,__ I hate to wake__ you up to say__ good-bye.
played a-round,__ I tell you now,__ they don't mean__ a thing.
me kiss you,__ then close your eyes,__ I'll be on__ my way.

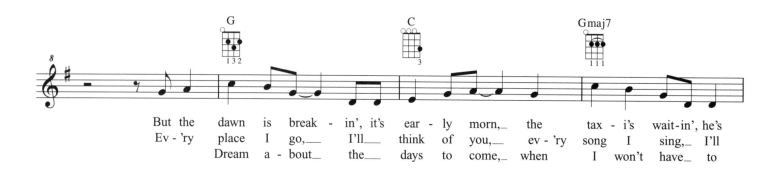

But the dawn is break-in', it's ear-ly morn,__ the tax-i's wait-in', he's
Ev-'ry place I go,__ I'll__ think of you,__ ev-'ry song I sing,__ I'll
Dream a-bout__ the__ days to come,__ when I won't have__ to

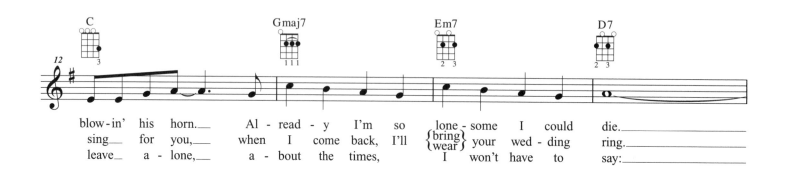

blow-in' his horn.__ Al-read-y I'm so lone-some I could die.__
sing__ for you, when I come back, I'll {bring}{wear} your wed-ding ring.__
leave__ a-lone,__ a-bout the times, I won't have to say:__

Leaving on a Jet Plane - 2 - 1

© 1967 (Renewed) RESERVOIR MEDIA MANAGEMENT, INC. and CHERRY LANE MUSIC PUBLISHING COMPANY, INC.
RESERVOIR MEDIA MANAGEMENT, INC. Administered by RESERVOIR MEDIA MANAGEMENT, INC.
RESERVOIR MEDIA MUSIC (ASCAP) Administered by ALFRED MUSIC
All Rights Reserved

Chorus:

MARGARITAVILLE

Use Suggested Strum Pattern #2

Moderately

Words and Music by
JIMMY BUFFETT

Intro:

Verse:

1. Nib-blin' on sponge - cake, watch-in' the sun___ bake;
2.3. *See additional lyrics*

all of those tour - ists cov-ered with oil.

Strum-min' my six___ string, on my front porch___ swing.

Smell those shrimp;___ they're be - gin-ning to boil.___

Chorus:

Wast-in' a - way a - gain___ in Mar - ga - ri - ta-ville,

search-in' for my_____ lost shak - er of salt.___

Some_ peo - ple claim___ that there's_ a wom - an to blame,_____ { but I know_
{ now I think,_
{ but I know

© 1977 (Renewed) CORAL REEFER MUSIC
All Rights Reserved

Verse 2:
Don't know the reason,
I stayed here all season
With nothing to show but this brand-new tattoo.
But it's a real beauty,
A Mexican cutie,
How it got here I haven't a clue.
(To Chorus:)

Verse 3
I blew out my flip-flop,
Stepped on a pop-top;
Cut my heel, had to cruise on back home.
But there's booze in the blender,
And soon it will render
That frozen concoction that helps me hang on.
(To Chorus:)

MARRY ME

Words and Music by
SAM HOLLANDER and PAT MONAHAN

Use Suggested Strum Pattern #2
Moderately
Verse:

1. For - ev - er could nev - er be long e - nough_ for me to
2. To - geth - er can nev - er be close e - nough_ for me to

feel like I've had long e - nough_ with you.
feel like I am close e - nough_ to you.

For -

get the world,_ now, we won't let them see.
You wear white and I'll_ wear out the words "I love_you"

But there's one thing left to do._
and "you're

Pre-chorus:

_ beau-ti-ful."
Now that the weight_ has lift - ed_
Now that the wait_ is o - ver_

and love has sure - ly_ shift - ed my way,_
and love has fi - n'lly_ showed_ her my way,_

Chorus:

mar - ry_ me
to - day_ and ev - 'ry_

_ day. Mar - ry_ me.

Marry Me - 2 - 1

© 2009 RESERVOIR MEDIA MANAGEMENT, INC. (IMRO), MAYDAY MALONE MUSIC (ASCAP), EMI APRIL MUSIC, INC. (ASCAP),
BLUE LAMP MUSIC (ASCAP), EMI BLACKWOOD MUSIC, INC. (BMI) and REPTILLIAN MUSIC (BMI)
All Rights for RESERVOIR MEDIA MUSIC (ASCAP) and MAYDAY MALONE MUSIC (ASCAP)
Administered by RESERVOIR MEDIA MANAGEMENT, INC.
RESERVOIR MEDIA MUSIC (ASCAP) Administered by ALFRED MUSIC
All Rights Reserved

81

Marry Me - 2 - 2

THEME FROM *NEW YORK, NEW YORK*

Words by
FRED EBB

Music by
JOHN KANDER

Use Suggested Strum Pattern #14
Moderately

Theme from New York, New York - 3 - 1

© 1977 (Renewed) UNITED ARTISTS CORPORATION
All Rights Controlled by EMI UNART CATALOG INC. (Publishing) and ALFRED MUSIC PUBLISHING CO., INC. (Print)
All Rights Reserved

84

OVER THE RAINBOW

Use Suggested
Strum Pattern #13
Moderate reggae feel

Music by HAROLD ARLEN
Lyrics by E.Y. HARBURG

© 1938 (Renewed) METRO-GOLDWYN-MAYER INC.
© 1939 (Renewed) EMI FEIST CATALOG INC.
All Rights Controlled and Administered by EMI FEIST CATALOG INC. (Publishing) and ALFRED MUSIC (Print)
All Rights Reserved

PAINT IT, BLACK

Words and Music by
MICK JAGGER and KEITH RICHARDS

Paint It, Black - 2 - 1

© 1966 (Renewed) ABKCO MUSIC, INC., 85 Fifth Avenue, New York, NY 10003
All Rights Reserved

Verse 3:
I look inside myself and see my heart is black.
I see my red door, I must have it painted black.

Bridge 3:
Maybe then I'll fade away and not have to face the facts.
It's not easy facing up when your whole world is black.

Verse 4:
No more will my green sea go turn a deeper blue.
I could not foresee this thing happening to you.

Bridge 4:
If I look hard enough into the setting sun,
My love will laugh with me before the mornin' comes.
(To Verse 5:)

PINBALL WIZARD

Use Suggested Strum Pattern #1

Words and Music by
PETER TOWNSHEND

© 1969 (Renewed) FABULOUS MUSIC LTD.
Published by FABULOUS MUSIC LTD.
Administered in the U.S. and Canada by SPIRIT ONE MUSIC (BMI) o/b/o SPIRIT SERVICES HOLDINGS, S.à.r.l.,
SUOLUBAF MUSIC and ABKCO MUSIC, INC., 85 Fifth Avenue, New York, NY 10003
International Copyright Secured   All Rights Reserved   Used by Permission

Pinball Wizard - 2 - 1

(WE'RE GONNA)
ROCK AROUND THE CLOCK

Use Suggested Strum Pattern #14
Moderately bright swing

Words and Music by
MAX C. FREEDMAN
and JIMMY DE KNIGHT

One, two, three-o-clock, four-o-clock rock. Five, six, sev'n o-clock, eight-o-clock rock.

Nine, ten, e-lev'n o-'clock, twelve-o-clock rock. We're gon-na rock a-round the

Verses 1 & 2:

clock to-night. 1. Put your glad rags on, join me, hon; we'll
(2.) clock strikes two, three and four, if the

have some fun when the clock strikes one. We're gon-na rock a-round the
band slows down, we'll yell for more. We're gon-na rock a-round the

clock to-night. We're gon-na rock, rock, rock 'til broad day-light. We're gon-na
clock to-night. We're gon-na rock, rock, rock 'til broad day-light. We're gon-na

rock, gon-na rock a-round___ the clock___ to-night.___
rock, gon-na rock a-round___ the clock___ to-night.___

1. | 2. | *Verses 3 & 4:*

2. When the 3. When the chimes ring five, six and sev-en,
eight, nine ten, e-lev-en too,___ I'll be

(We're Gonna) Rock Around the Clock - 2 - 1

© 1953 (Renewed) CAPANO MUSIC and MYERS MUSIC, INC. (c/o SONY/ATV MUSIC PUBLISHING LLC)
All Rights Reserved

ROCKY MOUNTAIN HIGH

Use Suggested Strum Pattern #6

Words and Music by
JOHN DENVER and MIKE TAYLOR

Rocky Mountain High - 3 - 1

© 1972 (Renewed) RESERVOIR MEDIA MUSIC (ASCAP), BMG RUBY SONGS (ASCAP) and WB MUSIC CORP. (ASCAP)
All Rights for RESERVOIR MEDIA MUSIC (ASCAP) Administered by RESERVOIR MEDIA MANAGEMENT, INC.
RESERVOIR MEDIA MUSIC (ASCAP) Administered by ALFRED MUSIC
All Rights Reserved

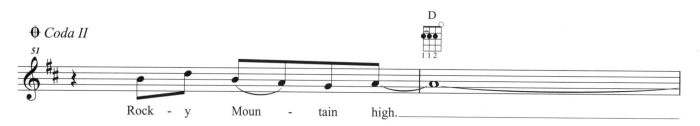

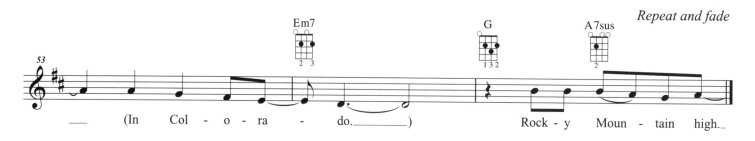

Verse 2:
When he first came to the mountains his life was far away,
On the road and hangin' by a song.
But the string's already broken and he doesn't really care.
It keeps changin' fast, and it don't last for long.
(To Chorus 1:)

Verse 3:
He climbed cathedral mountains, he saw silver clouds below.
He saw everything as far as you can see.
And they say that he got crazy once and he tried to touch the sun,
And he lost a friend but kept his memory.

Verse 4:
Now he walks in quiet solitude the forests and the streams,
Seeking grace in every step he takes.
His sight has turned inside himself to try and understand
The serenity of a clear blue mountain lake.

Chorus 2:
And the Colorado Rocky Mountain high,
I've seen it rainin' fire in the sky.
You can talk to God and listen to the casual reply.
Rocky Mountain high. (In Colorado.)
Rocky Mountain high. (In Colorado.)

Verse 5:
Now his life is full of wonder but his heart still knows some fear
Of a simple thing he cannot comprehend.
Why they try to tear the mountains down to bring in a couple more,
More people, more scars upon the land.

Chorus 3:
And the Colorado Rocky Mountain high,
I've seen it rainin' fire in the sky.
I know he'd be a poorer man if he never saw an eagle fly.
Rocky Mountain high.

Chorus 4:
It's a Colorado Rocky Mountain high.
I've seen it rainin' fire in the sky.
Friends around the campfire and everybody's high.
Rock Mountain high. (In Colorado.)

(I CAN'T GET NO) SATISFACTION

Use Suggested Strum Pattern #4
Moderately

Words and Music by
MICK JAGGER and KEITH RICHARDS

© 1965 (Renewed) ABKCO MUSIC, INC., 85 Fifth Avenue, New York, NY 10003
All Rights Reserved

Verse 2:
When I'm watchin' my TV,
And a man comes on and tells me
How white my shirts can be,
But he can't be a man 'cause he doesn't smoke
The same cigarettes as me.
I can't get no, oh, no, no, no.
Hey, hey, hey, that's what I say.
(To Chorus:)

Verse 3:
When I'm ridin' 'round the world,
And I'm doin' this and I'm signin' that,
And I'm tryin' to make some girl
Who tells me, baby, better come back maybe next week,
'Cause you see I'm on a losin' streak.
I can't get no, oh, no, no, no.
Hey, hey, hey, that's what I say.
I can't get no…
(To Outro:)

SHE LOVES YOU

Use Suggested Strum Pattern #2
Moderately bright

Words and Music by
JOHN LENNON and PAUL McCARTNEY

Intro:

She loves you, yeah, yeah, yeah.__ She loves you, yeah,

yeah, yeah.__ She loves you, yeah, yeah, yeah, yeah._____ 1. You

Verse:

think you've lost your love, well, I saw her yes - ter - day.__ It's
2.3. *See additional lyrics*

you she's think - ing of, and she told me what to say.__ She said she

loves you, and you know that can't be bad. Yes, she

loves you, and you know you should be glad.__ 2. She

Chorus:

Oo.__ She loves you, yeah, yeah, yeah.__ She

She Loves You - 2 - 1

© 1963 (Renewed) NORTHERN SONGS, LTD (PRS)
All Rights in the United States of America, its territories and possessions and Canada
Assigned to and Controlled by ROUND HILL WORKS (BMI) on behalf of GIL MUSIC CORP. (BMI)
All Rights Reserved

Verse 2:
She said you hurt her so she almost lost her mind.
But now she says she knows you're not the hurting kind.
She said she loves you and you know that can't be bad.
Yes, she loves you and you know you should be glad, oo.
(To Chorus:)

Verse 3:
You know it's up to you, I think it's only fair.
Pride can hurt you too, apologize to her.
Because she loves you and you know that can't be bad.
Yes, she loves you and you know you should be glad, oo.
(To Chorus:)

SHOWER THE PEOPLE

Use Suggested Strum Pattern #6

Moderately

Words and Music by
JAMES TAYLOR

© 1975 (Renewed) COUNTRY ROAD MUSIC, INC.
All Rights Reserved

SINGIN' IN THE RAIN

Lyric by
ARTHUR FREED

Music by
NACIO HERB BROWN

Use Suggested Strum Pattern #4

Moderately bright swing

A

G   G6   G

I'm sing - in' in the rain,   just sing - in' in the

G6   G   G6   G#dim7   Am7   D7

rain. What a glo - ri - ous feel - ing, I'm hap - py a - gain. I'm

Am7   D7   Am7   D7   Am7

laugh - ing at clouds so dark up a - bove, the sun's___ in my

D7   G   G6   G   G6

heart___ and I'm read - y for love. Let the storm - y clouds chase ev - 'ry -

G   G6   G   G6   G#dim7   Am7

one___ from the place. Come on___ with the rain, I've a smile___ on my

D7   Am7   D7   Am7   D7

face. I'll walk down the lane with a hap - py re - frain, and

Singin' in the Rain - 2 - 1

© 1929 (Renewed) METRO-GOLDWYN-MAYER INC.
All Rights Controlled and Administered by EMI ROBBINS CATALOG INC. (Publishing) and ALFRED MUSIC (Print)
All Rights Reserved

SON OF A SON OF A SAILOR

Words and Music by
JIMMY BUFFETT

Son of a Son of a Sailor - 2 - 1

©1978 CORAL REEFER MUSIC
All Rights Reserved

Verse 3:
Now away in the near future,
South-east of disorder,
You can shake the hand of the mango man
As he greets you at the border.

Verse 4:
And the lady she hails from Trinidad;
Island of the spices
Salt for your meat, and cinnamon sweet,
And the rum is for all your good vices.

Chorus 2:
Haul the sheet in as we ride on the wind
That our fore-fathers harnessed before us.
Hear the bells ring as the tide rigging sings.
It's a son of a gun of a chorus.

Verse 5:
Where it all ends I can't fathom, my friends.
If I knew, I might toss out my anchor.
So I'll cruise along always searchin' for songs,
Not a lawyer, a thief or a banker.
(To Chorus 3:)

SQUEEZE BOX

Use Suggested Strum Pattern #1

Moderately fast

Words and Music by
PETER TOWNSHEND

Squeeze Box - 2 - 1

© 1975 (Renewed) SPIRIT CATALOGUE HOLDINGS, S.à.r.l.
U.S., UK/Eire and Canadian Rights for SPIRIT CATALOGUE HOLDINGS, S.à.r.l. Controlled and Administered by SPIRIT ONE MUSIC (BMI)
Rights for the Rest of World are Controlled and Administered by SPIRIT SERVICES HOLDINGS, S.à.r.l. on behalf of SPIRIT CATALOGUE HOLDINGS, S.à.r.l.
International Copyright Secured   All Rights Reserved   Used by Permission

STAND BY YOUR MAN

Use Suggested Strum Pattern #4

Moderate country swing

Words and Music by
TAMMY WYNETTE and BILLY SHERRILL

© 1967 (Renewed) EMI AL GALLICO MUSIC CORP.
Exclusive Print Rights Administered by ALFRED MUSIC
All Rights Reserved

Stand by Your Man - 2 - 2

SUPERSTAR

Words and Music by
LEON RUSSELL, BONNIE BRAMLETT
and DELANEY BRAMLETT

Use Suggested Strum Pattern #6
Slowly

1. Long a - go and, oh, so far a - way
2. Lone - li - ness is such a sad af - fair,

I fell in love with you be - fore the
and I can hard - ly wait to be with

sec - ond show. Your gui - tar,
you a - gain. What to say

it sounds so sweet and clear, but you're not
to make you come a - gain, come back to

To Coda

real - ly here, it's just the ra - di - o.
me a - gain and play your sad gui - tar.

Superstar - 2 - 1

© 1971 (Renewed) RESERVOIR MEDIA MUSIC and EMBASSY MUSIC CORPORATION
All Rights for RESERVOIR MEDIA MUSIC Administered by RESERVOIR MEDIA MANAGEMENT
RESERVOIR MEDIA MANAGEMENT Administered by ALFRED MUSIC
All Rights Reserved

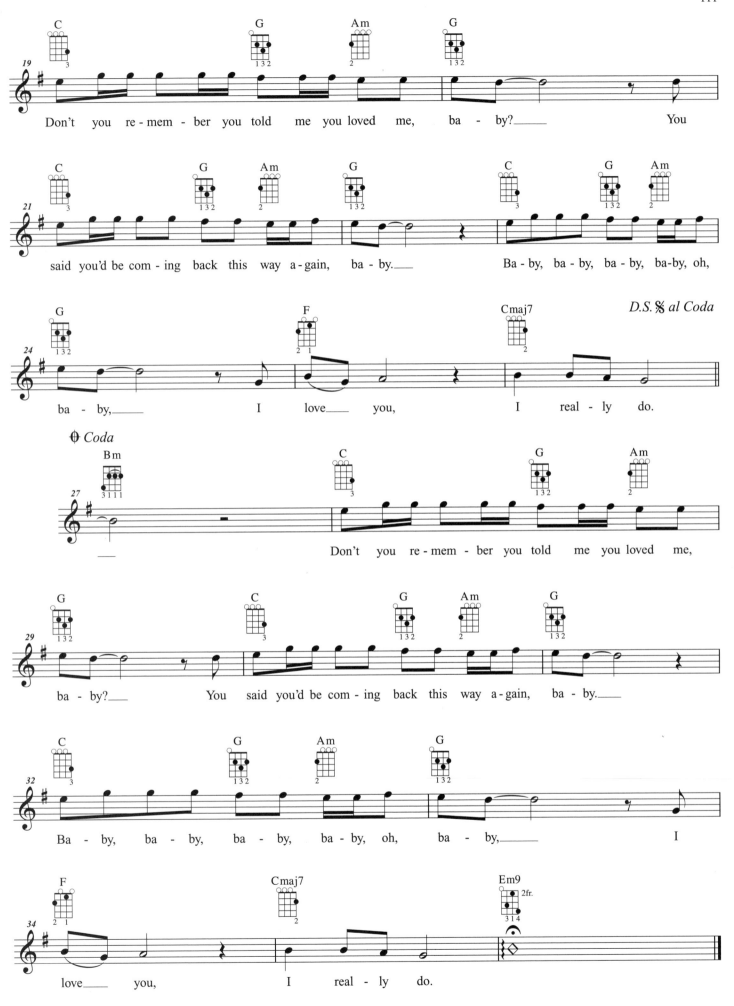

TAKE ME HOME, COUNTRY ROADS

Use Suggested Strum Pattern #3

Moderately bright

Words and Music by
JOHN DENVER, BILL DANOFF
and TAFFY NIVERT

Take Me Home, Country Roads - 2 - 1

© 1971 (Renewed) RESERVOIR MEDIA MANAGEMENT, INC., CHERRY LANE MUSIC PUBLISHING COMPANY, INC.,
ANNA KATE DEUTSCHENDORF, ZACHARY DEUTSCHENDORF and JESSE BELLE DENVER
All Rights for RESERVOIR MEDIA MUSIC Administered by RESERVOIR MEDIA MANAGEMENT, INC.
RESERVOIR MEDIA MUSIC Administered by ALFRED MUSIC
All Rights for ANNA KATE DEUTSCHENDORF and ZACHARY DEUTSCHENDORF Administered by CHERRY LANE MUSIC PUBLISHING COMPANY, INC.
All Rights for JESSE BELLE DENVER Administered by WB MUSIC CORP.
All Rights Reserved

TELL HER NO

Use Suggested Strum Pattern #6

Words and Music by
ROD ARGENT

© 1964 (Renewed) VERULAM MUSIC CO., LTD.
All Rights for the U.S. and Canada Controlled by MAINSTAY MUSIC, INC.
All Rights Reserved

Verse 2:
(me.) And if she should tell you, "I love you," whoa, whoa.
And if she tempts you with her charms…

Chorus 2:
Tell her no, no, no, no, no, no, no, no,
No, no, no, no, no, no, no, no.
Don't take her love from my arms.
No, no, no, no, no.
Don't hurt me now, for her love belongs to me.

Verse 3:
If she tells you, "I love you," whoa,
Just remember she said that to me.

Chorus 3:
Tell her no, no, no, no, no, no, no, no,
No, no, no, no, no, no, no, no.
Don't take her love from my arms.
No, no, no, no, no.
Don't leave me now, for her love belongs to me.

WHEN YOU'RE SMILING

Use Suggested Strum Pattern #14
Bright swing

Words and Music by
MARK FISHER, JOE GOODWIN
and LARRY SHAY

© 1928 (Renewed) EMI MILLS MUSIC INC. and MUSIC BY SHAY (c/o The Songwriters Guild of America)
Exclusive Print Rights for EMI MILLS MUSIC INC. Controlled and Administered by ALFRED MUSIC
All Rights Reserved

WOODSTOCK

Moderately

Intro:

Use Suggested Strum Pattern #6

Words and Music by
JONI MITCHELL

1. Well, I came_

Verse:

___ up - on___ a child___ of God, he was walk-ing a - long___ the road___ and___ I asked___

2.3. See additional lyrics

___ him, "Tell me where are you go - ing?" this he told___ me: said, "I'm go -

- ing down_ to Yas - gur's Farm,_ gon-na join___ in a rock and roll___ band._ Got to

get back to the land___ and set___ my soul___ free." We are star -

Chorus:

- dust, we are gold - en, we are bil - lion year old___ car - bon, and we got_

___ to get___ our - selves___ back to the gar -

Repeat ad lib. & fade

|1.2. ||3.

den. 2. Well, then den.

Verse 2:
Well, then can I walk beside you? I have come to lose the smog.
And I feel as if a cog in something turning.
And maybe it's the time of year, yes, and maybe it's the time of man.
And I don't know who I am but life is for learning.
(To Chorus:)

Verse 3:
By the time we got to Woodstock, we were half a million strong,
And everywhere was a song and a celebration.
And I dreamed I saw the bomber jet planes riding shotgun in the sky,
Turning into butterflies above our nation.
(To Chorus:)

© 1969 (Renewed) CRAZY CROW MUSIC
All Rights Administered by SONY/ATV MUSIC PUBLISHING, 8 Music Square West, Nashville, TN 37203
All Rights Reserved

YOU SEND ME

Use Suggested Strum Pattern #13

Moderately

Words and Music by
SAM COOKE

© 1957 (Renewed) ABKCO MUSIC, INC., 85 Fifth Avenue, New York, NY 10003
All Rights Reserved